Beef Stew with Olives & Raisins

Currant jelly, green olives, and raisins make this a uniquely different stew. For a change from Mom's old-fashioned beef stew, try this delicious variation.

2 tablespoons all-purpose flour

1 pound beef stew meat, cut into 1-inch cubes

2 tablespoons cooking oil

5 medium carrots, bias-sliced into ½-inch pieces

3 medium parsley roots or 2 medium parsnips, bias-sliced into ½-inch pieces

12 ounces boiling onions, peeled and halved

1 14½-ounce can beef broth

1 14½-ounce can tomatoes, cut up

2 tablespoons currant or apple jelly

2 cloves garlic, minced

1 bay leaf

1 tablespoon snipped fresh thyme or 1 teaspoon dried thyme, crushed

¼ teaspoon pepper

½ cup almond-stuffed green olives or pimiento-stuffed green olives

⅓ cup golden raisins

Place flour in a plastic bag. Add meat cubes, a few at a time, shaking to coat meat with flour. In a large skillet brown meat, half at a time, in hot oil. Drain off fat.

In a 3½- or 4-quart crockery cooker place carrots, parsley roots or parsnips, and onions. Add meat. In a bowl combine broth, undrained tomatoes, jelly, garlic, bay leaf, dried thyme (if using), and pepper. Pour over meat and vegetables.

Cover; cook on low-heat setting for 8 to 10 hours or on high-heat setting for 4 to 5 hours. Remove and discard bay leaf. To serve, stir in olives, raisins, and, if using, the fresh thyme.

Makes 4 servings • Prep time: 30 minutes

Nutrition facts per serving: 472 calories, 17 g total fat (4 g saturated fat), 82 mg cholesterol, 947 mg sodium, 51 mg carbohydrate, 8 g fiber, 34 g protein. Daily Values: 221% vitamin A, 46% vitamin C, 11% calcium, 40% iron.

There's nothing like a bowl of old-fashioned beef stew.
Served with corn bread or biscuits, this is a hearty,
comforting meal—ready when you walk in the door.

Old-Time Beef Stew

In a large skillet brown meat, half at a time, in hot oil. Drain off fat.

In a 3½-, 4-, or 5-quart crockery cooker place the carrots, potatoes, and onions. Add meat. Sprinkle with tapioca, Worcestershire sauce, salt, and pepper. Add bay leaves. Pour water over all.

Cover; cook on low-heat setting for 8 to 10 hours or on high-heat setting for 4 to 5 hours. Remove bay leaves. If desired, serve with warm corn bread or biscuits.

Makes 6 servings • Prep time: 30 minutes

Nutrition facts per serving: 329 calories, 11 g total fat (3 g saturated fat), 82 mg cholesterol, 320 mg sodium, 28 g carbohydrate, 3 g fiber, 29 g protein. Daily Values: 114% vitamin A, 29% vitamin C, 3% calcium, 27% iron.

1½ pounds beef stew meat, cut into 1-inch cubes

1 tablespoon cooking oil

4 medium carrots, cut into ¾-inch slices

3 medium potatoes, cut into 1-inch chunks

8 ounces boiling onions, peeled and halved, or ½ of a 16-ounce package (about 2 cups) frozen small whole onions

3 tablespoons quick-cooking tapioca

2 tablespoons Worcestershire sauce

½ teaspoon salt

¼ teaspoon pepper

2 bay leaves

3 cups water

Corn bread or biscuits (optional)

The Right Thyme

Timing is everything when it comes to adding herbs during cooking. If you use a dried herb, add it at the beginning of cooking. If you use a fresh herb, add it at the end of cooking.

If you add a fresh herb in the beginning, it will lose all of its flavor and color by the end of the long cooking time. Fresh rosemary, which can withstand long cooking times, is an exception.

Chili with Double Bean Toss

A two-bean salad makes this chili stand out from the rest. The lime-garlic-dressed salad adds a refreshing complement to this hearty chili soup.

1 pound boneless beef top round steak

1 tablespoon cooking oil

2 14½-ounce cans diced tomatoes

1 14½-ounce can beef broth

1 large onion, chopped

1 or 2 fresh jalapeño or serrano peppers, finely chopped

2 cloves garlic, minced

2 tablespoons cornmeal

4 teaspoons chili powder

1 tablespoon brown sugar

1½ teaspoons dried oregano, crushed

½ teaspoon ground cumin

¼ teaspoon black pepper

1 recipe Double Bean Toss

Dairy sour cream (optional)

Trim fat from meat. Thinly slice meat across the grain into bite-size pieces. In a large skillet brown meat, half at a time, in hot oil. Drain off fat.

In a 3½- or 4-quart crockery cooker combine undrained tomatoes, beef broth, onion, jalapeño or serrano peppers, garlic, cornmeal, chili powder, brown sugar, oregano, cumin, and black pepper. Stir in meat.

Cover; cook on low-heat setting for 10 to 12 hours or on high-heat setting for 5 to 6 hours. Serve chili in bowls with Double Bean Toss on the side. If desired, top with sour cream.

Makes 6 servings • Prep time: 25 minutes

Double Bean Toss: In a bowl combine one 15-ounce can pinto beans and one 15-ounce can black beans, rinsed and drained. Add ½ teaspoon finely shredded lime peel, 1 tablespoon lime juice, 1 tablespoon salad oil, and 1 clove garlic, minced. Toss to mix.

Nutrition facts per serving: 315 calories, 9 g total fat (2 g saturated fat), 48 mg cholesterol, 1,049 mg sodium, 33 g carbohydrate, 8 g fiber, 28 g protein. Daily Values: 14% vitamin A, 47% vitamin C, 9% calcium, 33% iron.

Beef & Pumpkin Soup

Pumpkin, plus a dash of nutmeg, lends a fall harvest flair to this pasta-filled soup. If fresh pumpkin isn't available, use butternut squash instead.

In a 3½-, 4-, or 5-quart crockery cooker combine meat, corn, pumpkin or squash, water, tomato sauce, onion, sweet pepper, garlic, salt, black pepper, and nutmeg.

Cover; cook on low-heat setting for 10 to 12 hours or on high-heat setting for 5 to 6 hours.

Cook pasta according to package directions; drain. Stir pasta into the soup. Ladle soup into bowls; sprinkle with parsley.

Makes 6 servings · Prep time: 20 minutes

Nutrition facts per serving: 301 calories, 9 g total fat (3 g saturated fat), 82 mg cholesterol, 467 mg sodium, 26 g carbohydrate, 2 g fiber, 31 g protein. Daily Values: 27% vitamin A, 32% vitamin C, 3% calcium, 29% iron.

1½ pounds beef stew meat, cut into 1-inch cubes

1 10-ounce package frozen whole kernel corn

1½ cups ½-inch pieces peeled and seeded pumpkin or butternut squash

1½ cups water

1 8-ounce can tomato sauce

¾ cup chopped onion

½ cup chopped green sweet pepper

1 clove garlic, minced

½ teaspoon salt

¼ teaspoon black pepper

⅛ teaspoon ground nutmeg

2 ounces dried medium shell macaroni or cavatelli

¼ cup snipped parsley

Here's a great way to use one of the best bargains you can find at the meat counter—pork shoulder. Often, this cut is on special, so take advantage of its value and flavor.

Pork & Sweet Potato Stew

1   pound boneless pork shoulder roast, cut into 1-inch cubes

1   tablespoon cooking oil

6   medium sweet potatoes (about 2 pounds), peeled and cut into 1-inch pieces

1   medium onion, coarsely chopped (1 cup)

⅓   cup dried apples, coarsely chopped

1   tablespoon quick-cooking tapioca

1   clove garlic, minced

2   teaspoons snipped fresh sage or ½ teaspoon dried sage, crushed

¼   teaspoon ground cardamom

¼   teaspoon pepper

2   cups chicken broth

1   cup apple juice or apple cider

In a large skillet brown meat, half at a time, in hot oil. Drain off fat.

In a 3½- or 4-quart crockery cooker place sweet potatoes, onion, and dried apples. Add meat. Sprinkle with tapioca, garlic, dried sage (if using), cardamom, and pepper. Pour broth and juice or cider over all.

Cover; cook on low-heat setting for 6 hours or on high-heat setting for 3 hours. If using, stir in the fresh sage.

Makes 6 servings • Prep time: 25 minutes

Nutrition facts per serving: 324 calories, 11 g total fat (3 g saturated fat), 50 mg cholesterol, 316 mg sodium, 40 g carbohydrate, 5 g fiber, 17 g protein. Daily Values: 257% vitamin A, 79% vitamin C, 4% calcium, 12% iron.

A Full Pot

Unlike cooking in a saucepan, the heat in a crockery cooker comes from coils that are wrapped around the sides of the pot. Therefore, a cooker that is at least half full will cook most efficiently.

When you remove the meat from the cooker, the juices will likely fill the cooker less than halfway. So, when thickening juices, thicken them in a saucepan rather than in the cooker.

Spicy Pork & Potato Stew

*Poblano peppers are mild to medium-hot. They're long
and deep green with an irregular bell-pepper shape.
Remove the membranes and seeds for the mildest flavor.*

In a large skillet brown meat, half at a time, in hot oil.
Drain off fat.

In a 3½- or 4-quart crockery cooker place potatoes,
onions, poblano peppers, jalapeño pepper, garlic, and
stick cinnamon. Add meat. In a bowl combine chicken
broth, undrained tomatoes, chili powder, oregano, and
black pepper; pour over all.

Cover; cook on low-heat setting for 8 to 10 hours or on
high-heat setting for 4 to 5 hours. Discard stick
cinnamon. Stir in cilantro or parsley. If desired, serve
stew over hot cooked rice.

Makes 6 servings • Prep time: 30 minutes

Nutrition facts per serving: 285 calories, 11 g total fat (3 g saturated fat), 50 mg cholesterol,
753 mg sodium, 28 g carbohydrate, 3 g fiber, 19 g protein. Daily Values: 12% vitamin A,
202% vitamin C, 5% calcium, 21% iron.

*Note: Because fresh chili peppers contain pungent oils
(the membranes and the seeds carry the heat), protect
your hands when handling fresh chili peppers. Wear
plastic gloves or put sandwich bags over your hands.
Always wash your hands and nails thoroughly in hot,
soapy water after handling chili peppers.

1 pound boneless pork shoulder
  roast, cut into 1-inch cubes

1 tablespoon cooking oil

1 pound whole, tiny new potatoes,
  quartered

2 medium onions, chopped

2 fresh poblano peppers, seeded
  and cut into 1-inch pieces*

1 fresh jalapeño pepper, seeded
  and chopped*

4 cloves garlic, minced

2 inches stick cinnamon

3 cups chicken broth

1 14½-ounce can diced tomatoes

1 tablespoon chili powder

1 teaspoon dried oregano, crushed

¼ teaspoon black pepper

¼ cup snipped cilantro or parsley
  Hot cooked basmati or long-
  grain rice (optional)

Lentils, Canadian bacon, and cheese-filled tortellini make this soup a hearty meal in itself. A small salad or breadsticks are all you need to round it out.

Lentil-Tortellini Soup

½ cup dry lentils

2 cups coarsely shredded carrots

1 large onion, finely chopped

4 ounces chopped cooked ham or Canadian-style bacon

2 cloves garlic, minced

2 tablespoons snipped fresh basil or 2 teaspoons dried basil, crushed

1½ tablespoons snipped fresh thyme or 1½ teaspoons dried thyme, crushed

¼ teaspoon pepper

5 cups reduced-sodium chicken broth

1 cup water

1 9-ounce package refrigerated cheese-filled tortellini

4 cups torn fresh spinach

Rinse lentils; drain. Place lentils in a 3½-, 4-, or 5-quart crockery cooker. Add the carrots, onion, ham or bacon, garlic, dried basil and thyme (if using), and pepper. Pour broth and water over all.

Cover; cook on low-heat setting for 6½ to 7 hours or on high-heat setting for 3¼ to 3½ hours. If using low-heat setting, turn to high-heat setting. Stir in tortellini. Cover and cook 30 minutes more. To serve, stir in spinach and, if using, the fresh basil and thyme.

Makes 6 servings • Prep time: 20 minutes

Nutrition facts per serving: 245 calories, 5 g total fat (1 g saturated fat), 30 mg cholesterol, 1,023 mg sodium, 35 g carbohydrate, 4 g fiber, 16 g protein. Daily Values: 222% vitamin A, 25% vitamin C, 12% calcium, 20% iron.

Split pea soup gets a flavor boost from curry and an added richness from cream. For optimum curry flavor, use fresh curry powder. If it's fragrant, it's probably fresh.

Curried Split Pea Soup

Rinse split peas; drain. Place drained peas in a 3½-, 4-, or 5-quart crockery cooker. Add the ham bone or pork hocks, onion, celery, carrot, curry powder, dried marjoram or thyme (if using), and bay leaf. Pour chicken broth over all.

Cover; cook on low-heat setting for 10 to 12 hours or on high-heat setting for 4 to 5 hours. Remove ham bone or pork hocks. When cool enough to handle, cut meat off bones; finely chop meat. Discard the bones and bay leaf.

Return meat to crockery cooker. Stir in half-and-half or light cream and, if using, the fresh marjoram or thyme. Season to taste with salt and pepper.

Makes 5 servings • Prep time: 20 minutes

Nutrition facts per serving: 369 calories, 10 g total fat (5 g saturated fat), 38 mg cholesterol, 1,381 mg sodium, 43 g carbohydrate, 5 g fiber, 29 g protein. Daily Values: 101% vitamin A, 11% vitamin C, 11% calcium, 26% iron.

1¼ cups dry green split peas

1 small meaty ham bone or 2 smoked pork hocks

1 cup coarsely chopped onion

1 cup coarsely chopped celery

1 cup coarsely chopped carrot

1 tablespoon curry powder

1 tablespoon snipped fresh marjoram or thyme or 1 teaspoon dried marjoram or thyme, crushed

1 bay leaf

5 cups chicken broth

1 cup half-and-half or light cream

Salt

Pepper

Lamb & Barley Stew with Mint

Pearl barley adds a slightly chewy texture to this stew. "Pearl" refers to the polishing process of the hulled grain. It is sold in regular and quick-cooking forms.

1½ pounds lamb stew meat, cut into 1-inch cubes

2 tablespoons cooking oil

1 medium onion, chopped

4 cloves garlic, minced

2½ cups chicken broth

1 14½-ounce can diced tomatoes

½ cup pearl barley (regular)

¼ cup dry white wine (optional)

2 tablespoons snipped fresh dill or 1½ teaspoons dried dillweed

½ teaspoon salt

¼ teaspoon black pepper

1½ 7-ounce jars roasted red sweet peppers, drained and thinly sliced (about 1½ cups)

¼ cup snipped fresh mint

In a large skillet brown half of the meat in hot oil; remove meat from skillet. Add remaining meat, onion, and garlic. Cook until meat is brown and onion is tender. Drain off fat.

In a 3½-, 4-, or 5-quart crockery cooker combine the broth, undrained tomatoes, barley, wine (if desired), dried dillweed (if using), salt, and black pepper. Stir in the meat mixture.

Cover; cook on low-heat setting for 8 to 10 hours or on high-heat setting for 4 to 5 hours. To serve, stir in the roasted peppers and fresh mint. If using, stir in the fresh dill.

Makes 6 servings • Prep time: 20 minutes

Nutrition facts per serving: 266 calories, 11 g total fat (3 g saturated fat), 58 mg cholesterol, 709 mg sodium, 19 g carbohydrate, 4 g fiber, 23 g protein. Daily Values: 23% vitamin A, 193% vitamin C, 3% calcium, 24% iron.

Chicken & Garbanzo Bean Soup

Fennel has a creamy white bulblike base, pale green stalks, and feathery green leaves. It has a light, licorice flavor and a texture that is similar to celery.

Rinse the garbanzo beans; place in a large saucepan. Add enough water to cover the beans by 2 inches. Bring to boiling; reduce heat. Simmer, uncovered, for 10 minutes. Remove from heat. Cover and let stand for 1 hour. (Or, place beans in water in a large saucepan. Cover and let soak in a cool place overnight.) Drain and rinse beans.

Rinse chicken. Place chicken and beans in a 3½-, 4-, or 5-quart crockery cooker. Add carrots, fennel or celery, onion, dried marjoram and thyme (if using), bouillon granules, salt, and pepper. Pour water over all.

Cover; cook on low-heat setting for 8 to 10 hours or on high-heat setting for 4 to 5 hours. Remove the chicken; cool slightly. Cut the meat into bite-size pieces. Return to cooker. Add the spinach or escarole and, if using, the fresh marjoram and thyme. Let stand 5 minutes before serving.

Makes 6 servings • Soak time: 1 hour • Prep time: 20 minutes

Nutrition facts per serving: 205 calories, 4 g total fat (1 g saturated fat), 40 mg cholesterol, 625 mg sodium, 23 g carbohydrate, 9 g fiber, 20 g protein. Daily Values: 149% vitamin A, 12% vitamin C, 6% calcium, 18% iron.

1   cup dry garbanzo beans

1   pound skinless, boneless chicken breasts or thighs

2½ cups sliced carrots

1   medium fennel bulb, trimmed and cut into ¼-inch slices, or 1½ cups sliced celery

1   large onion, chopped

1   tablespoon snipped fresh marjoram or 1 teaspoon dried marjoram, crushed

1   tablespoon snipped fresh thyme or 1 teaspoon dried thyme, crushed

1   tablespoon instant chicken bouillon granules

¼   teaspoon salt

¼   teaspoon pepper

4   cups water

1   cup shredded fresh spinach or escarole

Pot Roast with Basil Mashed Potatoes

What could be more comforting on a chilly day than a hearty, melt-in-your-mouth pot roast? Mashed potatoes combined with fresh basil add a special touch.

2 carrots, cut into ½-inch pieces

1 medium turnip, peeled and cubed (1 cup)

1 small onion, chopped

½ cup snipped dried tomatoes (not oil-packed)

1 clove garlic, minced

1 teaspoon instant beef bouillon granules

½ teaspoon dried basil, crushed

½ teaspoon dried oregano, crushed

⅛ teaspoon pepper

1 1½- to 2-pound boneless beef chuck pot roast

1 cup water

1 10-ounce package frozen lima beans or whole kernel corn

1 cup frozen peas

1 20-ounce package refrigerated mashed potatoes

1 tablespoon finely snipped fresh basil

In a 3½- or 4-quart crockery cooker combine the carrots, turnip, onion, dried tomatoes, garlic, bouillon granules, dried basil, dried oregano, and pepper. Trim fat from meat. If necessary, cut roast to fit into cooker. Place meat on top of vegetables. Pour water over all.

Cover; cook on low-heat setting for 8 to 10 hours or on high-heat setting for 4 to 5 hours. Stir in lima beans or corn and peas. Let stand, covered, for 10 minutes.

Meanwhile, prepare mashed potatoes according to package directions, except stir the 1 tablespoon fresh basil into potatoes just before serving. Remove meat and vegetables from cooker with a slotted spoon. If desired, reserve cooking juices. Serve meat and vegetables over hot mashed potatoes. If desired, serve cooking juices over meat.

Makes 6 servings • Prep time: 25 minutes

Nutrition facts per serving: 436 calories, 12 g total fat (5 g saturated fat), 87 mg cholesterol, 497 mg sodium, 46 g carbohydrate, 8 g fiber, 35 g protein. Daily Values: 55% vitamin A, 12% vitamin C, 4% calcium, 34% iron.

Southerners eat black-eyed peas on New Year's Day to ensure good luck throughout the year. Try them yourself —in southern style—with warm corn bread.

Pork Hocks & Black-Eyed Peas

Rinse black-eyed peas; place in a large saucepan. Add enough water to cover peas by 2 inches. Bring to boiling; reduce heat. Simmer, uncovered, for 10 minutes. Remove from heat. Cover and let stand for 1 hour. Drain and rinse peas.

In a 3½-, 4-, or 5-quart crockery cooker combine the black-eyed peas, pork hocks, broth, sweet pepper, onion, celery, bay leaves, and red pepper.

Cover; cook on low-heat setting for 8 to 10 hours or on high-heat setting for 4 to 5 hours. Add okra. Cover; let stand for 10 minutes or until okra is tender. Remove pork hocks. When cool enough to handle, cut meat off bones; cut meat into bite-size pieces. Discard bones and bay leaves. To serve, stir meat into black-eyed pea mixture.

Makes 6 servings • Soaking time: 1 hour • Prep time: 25 minutes

Nutrition facts per serving: 191 calories, 3 g total fat (1 g saturated fat), 14 mg cholesterol, 763 mg sodium, 28 g carbohydrate, 7 g fiber, 15 g protein. Daily Values: 4% vitamin A, 32% vitamin C, 5% calcium, 20% iron.

1½ cups dry black-eyed peas

4 small smoked pork hocks (1½ pounds)

4 cups reduced-sodium chicken broth

1 medium green sweet pepper, chopped

1 medium onion, chopped

1 stalk celery, chopped

2 bay leaves

¼ teaspoon ground red pepper

2 cups sliced okra or one 10-ounce package frozen whole okra, thawed and cut into ½-inch slices

Spiced Fruit & Chops with Couscous

Sweet and spicy describes this pork dish. Raisins, dried apples, and orange juice all contribute to the sweet flavor while a jalapeño pepper supplies the heat.

4 pork sirloin chops, cut ¾ inch thick (about 1½ pounds)

¼ teaspoon salt

¼ teaspoon black pepper

1 tablespoon cooking oil

1 6-ounce package dried apples

1 medium onion, chopped

¼ cup golden raisins

¾ cup orange juice

¾ cup chicken broth

1 small jalapeño pepper, seeded and finely chopped

1 clove garlic, minced

1 teaspoon grated gingerroot

½ teaspoon apple pie spice

  Chicken broth

¼ cup water

2 teaspoons cornstarch

1 recipe Orange-Almond Couscous

Sprinkle chops with salt and black pepper. In a large skillet cook chops in hot oil until brown, turning once. Transfer chops to a 3½- or 4-quart crockery cooker. Sprinkle apples, onion, and raisins over chops. In a bowl stir together orange juice, broth, jalapeño pepper, garlic, gingerroot, and apple pie spice. Pour over all.

Cover; cook on low-heat setting for 6 to 8 hours or on high-heat setting for 3 to 4 hours. Transfer chops and fruit to a platter; keep warm. For sauce, measure juices; skim fat from juices. If necessary, add broth to juices to make 1 cup. Place in a saucepan. Combine the ¼ cup water and the cornstarch; stir into juices in pan. Cook and stir until thickened. Cook and stir 2 minutes more. Serve chops and fruit with Orange-Almond Couscous. Pass sauce.

Makes 4 servings · Prep time: 20 minutes

Orange-Almond Couscous: In a saucepan bring 1 cup water and ¼ teaspoon salt to boiling. Remove from heat. Stir in ⅔ cup quick-cooking couscous and 1 teaspoon finely shredded orange peel. Cover; let stand 5 minutes. Stir in 2 tablespoons toasted slivered almonds.

Nutrition facts per serving: 462 calories, 12 g total fat (3 g saturated fat), 48 mg cholesterol, 531 mg sodium, 70 g carbohydrate, 11 g fiber, 22 g protein. Daily Values: 1% vitamin A, 55% vitamin C, 4% calcium, 15% iron.

Tomato-Sauced Pork Ribs

There are no bones about it. These boneless pork ribs, cooked in a rich tomato sauce, make perfect partners for a mound of hot noodles. Grab extra napkins!

For sauce, in a 3½- or 4-quart crockery cooker combine undrained tomatoes, celery, sweet pepper, onion, tapioca, sugar, dried basil (if using), salt, black pepper, hot pepper sauce, and garlic. Add ribs; stir to coat ribs with sauce.

Cover; cook on low-heat setting for 8 to 10 hours or on high-heat setting for 4 to 5 hours.

Transfer meat to a serving platter. Skim fat from sauce. If using, stir fresh basil into sauce. Spoon some of the sauce over meat. Serve with hot cooked noodles. Pass remaining sauce.

Makes 6 servings • Prep time: 20 minutes

Nutrition facts per serving: 314 calories, 20 g total fat (8 g saturated fat), 79 mg cholesterol, 477 mg sodium, 12 g carbohydrate, 2 g fiber, 21 g protein. Daily Values: 9% vitamin A, 52% vitamin C, 6% calcium, 15% iron.

- 1 28-ounce can crushed tomatoes
- 2 stalks celery, chopped
- 1 medium green sweet pepper, chopped
- 1 medium onion, chopped
- 2 tablespoons quick-cooking tapioca
- 1½ teaspoons sugar
- 1½ teaspoons snipped fresh basil or ½ teaspoon dried basil, crushed
- ½ teaspoon salt
- ¼ teaspoon black pepper
- ¼ teaspoon bottled hot pepper sauce
- 1 clove garlic, minced
- 2 pounds boneless pork country-style ribs
- 3 cups hot cooked noodles

Chicken Merlot with Mushrooms

*To ensure proper doneness, always place ingredients
in your crockery cooker in the order given in the recipe.
Generally, vegetables are added first and the meat is last.*

2½ to 3 pounds meaty chicken
pieces (breasts, thighs, and
drumsticks), skinned

3 cups sliced fresh mushrooms

1 large onion, chopped

2 cloves garlic, minced

¾ cup chicken broth

1 6-ounce can tomato paste

¼ cup dry red wine (such as
Merlot) or chicken broth

2 tablespoons quick-cooking
tapioca

2 tablespoons snipped fresh basil
or 1½ teaspoons dried basil,
crushed

2 teaspoons sugar

¼ teaspoon salt

¼ teaspoon pepper

2 cups hot cooked noodles

2 tablespoons finely shredded
Parmesan cheese

Rinse chicken; set aside. In a 3½-, 4-, or 5-quart
crockery cooker place mushrooms, onion, and garlic.
Place chicken pieces on top of the vegetables. In a
bowl combine broth, tomato paste, wine or chicken
broth, tapioca, dried basil (if using), sugar, salt, and
pepper. Pour over all.

Cover; cook on low-heat setting for 7 to 8 hours or on
high-heat setting for 3½ to 4 hours. If using, stir in
fresh basil. To serve, spoon chicken, mushroom
mixture, and sauce over hot cooked noodles. Sprinkle
with Parmesan cheese.

Makes 4 to 6 servings · Prep time: 25 minutes

Nutrition facts per serving: 469 calories, 12 g total fat (3 g saturated fat), 144 mg cholesterol,
468 mg sodium, 41 g carbohydrate, 5 g fiber, 46 g protein. Daily Values: 13% vitamin A,
37% vitamin C, 7% calcium, 35% iron.

Lamb Ragout with Couscous

Ragout (rah-goo) is a French term for a rich stew that contains meat, vegetables, and wine. With lamb, artichoke hearts, and zucchini, this stew is fit for any royal guests.

In a large skillet brown meat, half at a time, in hot oil. Drain off fat. Transfer meat to a 3½-, 4-, or 5-quart crockery cooker. Add the onion, tomatoes, carrots, and garlic. Sprinkle with tapioca. Combine beef broth, wine or water, Italian seasoning or oregano, salt, and pepper. Pour over all. Stir to combine.

Cover; cook on low-heat setting for 8 to 10 hours or on high-heat setting for 4 to 5 hours.

If using low-heat setting, turn to high-heat setting. Stir in the zucchini and thawed artichoke hearts. Cover; cook for 30 minutes more. Serve over couscous or rice.

Makes 6 servings • Prep time: 30 minutes

Nutrition facts per serving: 373 calories, 8 g total fat (3 g saturated fat), 61 mg cholesterol, 456 mg sodium, 47 g carbohydrate, 6 g fiber, 28 g protein. Daily Values: 59% vitamin A, 37% vitamin C, 6% calcium, 23% iron.

1½ to 2 pounds lamb stew meat, cut into 1-inch cubes

1 tablespoon cooking oil

2 cups coarsely chopped onion

2 medium tomatoes, chopped

2 medium carrots, cut into ½-inch slices

3 cloves garlic, minced

2 tablespoons quick-cooking tapioca

1 cup beef broth

¼ cup dry red wine or water

1 teaspoon dried Italian seasoning or oregano, crushed

½ teaspoon salt

¼ teaspoon pepper

2 small zucchini, halved lengthwise and cut into ¼-inch-thick slices

1 9-ounce package frozen artichoke hearts, thawed and quartered

3 cups hot cooked couscous or rice

Citrus Corned Beef Sandwiches

*Marinated corned beef is convenient to have on hand because,
when refrigerated, it has a shelf life of several weeks.
Add a few ingredients for these satisfying sandwiches.*

1   2- to 3-pound corned beef brisket with spice packet

1   cup water

¼   cup Dijon-style mustard

¼   teaspoon finely shredded orange peel (optional)

⅓   cup orange juice

4   teaspoons all-purpose flour

8   kaiser rolls, split

6   ounces sliced Muenster cheese

Trim fat from meat. Rub brisket with spices from spice packet. If necessary, cut the brisket to fit into a 3½-, 4-, or 5-quart crockery cooker. Place brisket in cooker. Combine water and mustard; pour over brisket.

Cover; cook on low-heat setting for 8 to 10 hours or on high-heat setting for 4 to 5 hours. Remove meat; cover to keep warm. Skim fat from juices. Reserve juices; discard whole spices. In a small saucepan stir together orange peel (if desired), orange juice, and flour; gradually stir in ¼ cup of the reserved cooking juices. Cook and stir until thickened and bubbly. Cook and stir 1 minute more.

Thinly slice meat across the grain. Arrange rolls, cut side up, on the unheated rack of a broiler pan. Broil 3 inches from heat for 1 to 2 minutes or until toasted. Remove roll tops from broiler pan. Place sliced meat on roll bottoms. Drizzle about 1 tablespoon of cooking juices over meat. Top with cheese. Broil 1 to 2 minutes more or until cheese melts. Add roll tops.

Makes 8 servings • Prep time: 30 minutes

Nutrition facts per serving: 464 calories, 24 g total fat (9 g saturated fat), 99 mg cholesterol, 1,539 mg sodium, 33 g carbohydrate, 0 g fiber, 26 g protein. Daily Values: 7% vitamin A, 30% vitamin C, 17% calcium, 23% iron.

Serve open-faced steak sandwiches with a culinary twist, just like your favorite bistro. Focaccia bread is available at many bakeries and larger supermarkets.

Ratatouille Steak Sandwiches

Trim fat from meat. Sprinkle both sides of meat with Italian seasoning, salt, and black pepper. If necessary, cut meat to fit into a 3½- or 4-quart crockery cooker. Place mushrooms, onion, and garlic in cooker. Add meat. Pour undrained tomatoes and vinegar over all.

Cover; cook on low-heat setting for 7 to 9 hours or on high-heat setting for 3½ to 4½ hours. If using low-heat setting, turn to high-heat setting. Add squash or zucchini and sweet peppers to cooker. Cover; cook on high-heat setting for 30 minutes more.

Remove meat from cooker. Stir in drained artichoke hearts. Thinly slice meat across grain. Arrange meat on the focaccia. Using a slotted spoon, place vegetable mixture over meat. Drizzle with a little of the cooking liquid. Sprinkle with cheese. To serve, cut into wedges.

Makes 6 to 8 servings •
Prep time: 20 minutes

Nutrition facts per serving: 440 calories, 15 g total fat (5 g saturated fat), 58 mg cholesterol, 369 mg sodium, 46 g carbohydrate, 4 g fiber, 34 g protein. Daily Values: 8% vitamin A, 52% vitamin C, 14% calcium, 25% iron.

1½ pounds beef flank steak
1 teaspoon dried Italian seasoning, crushed
Salt
Black pepper
1½ cups sliced fresh mushrooms
1 medium onion, finely chopped
2 cloves garlic, minced
1 14½-ounce can tomatoes, cut up
2 tablespoons red wine vinegar
1 medium yellow summer squash or zucchini, halved lengthwise and cut into ¼-inch-thick slices
1 cup green, red, and/or yellow sweet pepper strips
1 6-ounce jar marinated artichoke hearts, drained and halved
Purchased focaccia (about a 9-inch round)
⅓ cup finely shredded Asiago or Parmesan cheese

Barbecued Beef Sandwiches

Since beef brisket needs long, slow cooking to become tender, we recommend that you use the low-heat setting on your crockery cooker for this recipe.

1 2½- to 3-pound fresh beef brisket

1 10-ounce can chopped tomatoes with green chili peppers

1 8-ounce can applesauce

½ of a 6-ounce can (⅓ cup) tomato paste

¼ cup soy sauce

¼ cup packed brown sugar

1 tablespoon Worcestershire sauce

10 to 12 hamburger buns, split and toasted

Trim fat from meat. If necessary, cut meat to fit into a 3½-, 4-, or 5-quart crockery cooker. Place meat in cooker. In a bowl stir together the undrained tomatoes, applesauce, tomato paste, soy sauce, brown sugar, and Worcestershire sauce; pour over meat.

Cover; cook on low-heat setting about 10 hours or until meat is tender. Remove meat, reserving juices; cover to keep warm.

Pour cooking juices into a large saucepan. Bring to boiling; reduce heat. Boil gently, uncovered, for 15 to 20 minutes or until reduced to desired consistency, stirring frequently. Thinly slice meat across the grain. Place meat on bun bottoms. Drizzle with cooking juices; add bun tops.

Makes 10 to 12 servings • Prep time: 30 minutes

Nutrition facts per serving: 309 calories, 12 g total fat (4 g saturated fat), 78 mg cholesterol, 661 mg sodium, 23 g carbohydrate, 1 g fiber, 27 g protein. Daily Values: 3% vitamin A, 14% vitamin C, 3% calcium, 24% iron.

Jerk Pork Sandwiches with Lime Mayo

Mango, onions, and sweet pepper balance the flavor of the jerk seasoning. Serve with purchased sweet potato chips for a change from potato chips.

Trim fat from meat. Rub jerk seasoning evenly over roast. Place meat in a 3½- or 4-quart crockery cooker. Sprinkle with the thyme. Pour water over roast.

Cover; cook on low-heat setting for 8 to 10 hours or on high-heat setting for 4 to 5 hours. Remove meat from cooker, reserving juices. Shred meat, discarding any fat. Skim fat from juices. Add enough of the juices to moisten meat (about ½ cup). Stir lime juice into meat.

To serve, use a slotted spoon to place pork mixture onto roll bottoms. If desired, layer with lettuce leaves, sweet pepper rings, and mango slices. Spoon Lime Mayo onto each sandwich; add roll tops.

Makes 6 to 8 servings • Prep time: 30 minutes

Lime Mayo: In a bowl stir together ½ cup light mayonnaise dressing or regular mayonnaise, ¼ cup finely chopped red onion, ¼ teaspoon finely shredded lime peel, 1 tablespoon lime juice, and 1 clove garlic, minced. Cover; chill until ready to serve.

Nutrition facts per serving: 430 calories, 21 g total fat (6 g saturated fat), 74 mg cholesterol, 609 mg sodium, 34 g carbohydrate, 0 g fiber, 26 g protein. Daily Values: 4% vitamin A, 4% vitamin C, 6% calcium, 22% iron.

1 1½- to 2-pound boneless pork shoulder roast

1 tablespoon Jamaican jerk seasoning

¼ teaspoon dried thyme, crushed

1 cup water

1 tablespoon lime juice

6 to 8 kaiser rolls, split and toasted

6 to 8 lettuce leaves (optional)

6 thinly sliced red or green sweet pepper rings (optional)

1 medium mango, peeled and thinly sliced (optional)

1 recipe Lime Mayo

Mafalda with Sausage & Mushrooms

Mafalda is a long narrow or medium-width noodle with ruffled edges and resembles a lasagna noodle. If you can't find it, use fettuccine or spaghetti instead.

12 ounces bulk sweet Italian sausage

2 cups sliced fresh cremini and/or button mushrooms

1 28-ounce can crushed tomatoes

1 8-ounce can tomato sauce

1 6-ounce can tomato paste

⅔ cup water

1 medium onion, chopped

1 tablespoon sugar

1 teaspoon dried rosemary, crushed, or 1 tablespoon snipped fresh rosemary

¼ teaspoon pepper

2 cloves garlic, minced

9 to 12 ounces dried mafalda, fettuccine, or spaghetti

Freshly shredded or grated Parmesan cheese (optional)

In a large skillet brown sausage. Drain off fat. In a 3½- or 4-quart crockery cooker combine mushrooms, tomatoes, tomato sauce, tomato paste, water, onion, sugar, rosemary, pepper, and garlic. Stir in sausage.

Cover; cook on low-heat setting for 6 to 8 hours or on high-heat setting for 3 to 4 hours.

Just before serving, cook pasta according to package directions; drain. Serve sausage mixture over pasta. If desired, sprinkle with Parmesan cheese.

Makes 6 to 8 servings • Prep time: 15 minutes

Nutrition facts per serving: 358 calories, 10 g total fat (3 g saturated fat), 22 mg cholesterol, 938 mg sodium, 54 g carbohydrate, 4 g fiber, 14 g protein. Daily Values: 19% vitamin A, 47% vitamin C, 4% calcium, 28% iron.

Sancocho Pork Stew

This hearty stew, with its origin attributed to Panama, is mildly spiced with chili powder and chili peppers. The yams or sweet potatoes lend a complementary sweetness.

In a 3½-, 4-, or 5-quart crockery cooker place yams or sweet potatoes, sweet pepper, corn, onion, and garlic. Add pork, chili powder, coriander, and salt. Pour the water and the undrained tomatoes over all.

Cover; cook on low-heat setting for 7 to 8 hours or on high-heat setting for 3½ to 4 hours, adding the frozen green beans the last 15 minutes of cooking time.

Makes 6 to 8 servings • Prep time: 20 minutes

Nutrition facts per serving: 299 calories, 12 g total fat (4 g saturated fat), 74 mg cholesterol, 446 mg sodium, 26 g carbohydrate, 3 g fiber, 23 g protein. Daily Values: 135% vitamin A, 54% vitamin C, 5% calcium, 14% iron.

3 medium yams or sweet potatoes, peeled and cut into 2-inch pieces

1 large green sweet pepper, cut into strips

1 cup frozen whole kernel corn

1 medium onion, sliced and separated into rings

3 cloves garlic, minced

1½ pounds boneless pork shoulder, cut into ¾-inch cubes

1 teaspoon chili powder

¾ teaspoon ground coriander

½ teaspoon salt

2 cups water

1 10-ounce can chopped tomatoes with green chili peppers

1 9-ounce package frozen cut green beans

Old World Chicken

Juniper berries, native to Europe and America, add an intriguing flavor to this dish. The berries are popular in marinades and sauces and are used in making gin.

- 2 slices bacon
- 2½ to 3 pounds meaty chicken pieces (breasts, thighs, and drumsticks), skinned
- 1 teaspoon whole juniper berries
- 3 medium carrots, cut into ½-inch pieces
- ¼ cup chopped shallots or onions
- ¼ cup coarsely chopped celery
- ½ cup chicken broth
- ¼ cup dry red wine or port
- 2 tablespoons quick-cooking tapioca
- 1½ teaspoons snipped fresh thyme or ½ teaspoon dried thyme, crushed
- 1 teaspoon snipped fresh rosemary or ¼ teaspoon dried rosemary, crushed
- ¼ teaspoon salt
- ⅛ teaspoon pepper
- 1 cup frozen peas
- 2 tablespoons currant jelly
- 2 cups hot cooked rice

In a small skillet cook bacon until crisp; drain on paper towels. Crumble bacon; set aside. Rinse chicken; set aside. For spice bag, place juniper berries on a double-thick, 6-inch square of 100 percent cotton cheesecloth. Bring corners together and tie with clean cotton string.

In a 3½-, 4-, or 5-quart crockery cooker place carrots, shallots or onion, celery, and spice bag. Add chicken. Sprinkle with bacon. In a small bowl combine broth, wine or port, tapioca, dried thyme and rosemary (if using), salt, and pepper. Pour over all.

Cover; cook on low-heat setting for 6 to 7 hours or on high-heat setting for 3 to 3½ hours or until chicken is tender. Using a slotted spoon, transfer chicken and carrots to a serving platter; keep warm. If using low-heat setting, turn to high-heat setting. Stir in the peas and, if using, the fresh thyme and rosemary. Cook for 5 minutes more. Remove spice bag. Skim fat. Add currant jelly; stir until smooth. Pour over chicken mixture. Serve with hot cooked rice.

Makes 4 servings · Prep time: 30 minutes

Nutrition facts per serving: 474 calories, 11 g total fat (3 g saturated fat), 118 mg cholesterol, 500 mg sodium, 45 g carbohydrate, 3 g fiber, 43 g protein. Daily Values: 144% vitamin A, 11% vitamin C, 5% calcium, 25% iron.

Greek Chicken & Orzo

Feta cheese and olives add Greek flair to this meal. If you want the ultimate Greek touch, use Greek kalamata olives, which have a salty, rich, and fruity flavor.

Skin chicken. Rinse chicken; pat dry. In a large skillet brown chicken breasts in hot oil. In a 3½- or 4-quart crockery cooker combine fennel, onion, and garlic. Add the chicken breasts. In a bowl stir together water, balsamic vinegar, bouillon granules, dried oregano (if using), and crushed red pepper. Pour over all.

Cover; cook on low-heat setting for 5 to 6 hours or on high-heat setting for 2½ to 3 hours. If using, stir in the 1 tablespoon fresh oregano.

Cook the orzo according to package directions; drain. Stir tomato, cheese, olives, and the 1 tablespoon fresh oregano into orzo. Using a slotted spoon, remove chicken and vegetables from cooker. Serve with orzo mixture.

Makes 4 servings • Prep time: 25 minutes

Nutrition facts per serving: 439 calories, 12 g total fat (3 g saturated fat), 58 mg cholesterol, 626 mg sodium, 53 g carbohydrate, 13 g fiber, 28 g protein. Daily Values: 5% vitamin A, 22% vitamin C, 8% calcium, 24% iron.

4 medium chicken breast halves (about 1½ pounds total)

2 tablespoons cooking oil

1 medium fennel bulb, cut into ½-inch pieces (2 cups)

1 medium onion, cut into wedges

2 cloves garlic, minced

2 cups water

2 tablespoons white balsamic vinegar

2 teaspoons instant chicken bouillon granules

1 tablespoon snipped fresh oregano or 1 teaspoon dried oregano, crushed

¼ teaspoon crushed red pepper

1⅓ cups orzo pasta (rosamarina)

1 medium tomato, chopped

¼ cup crumbled feta cheese (1 ounce)

¼ cup chopped pitted ripe olives

1 tablespoon snipped fresh oregano

Cherry Gingerbread with Lemon Cream

Gingerbread gets a '90s update. Crystallized ginger and dried cherries give it a sophisticated flavor. The lemon whipped cream dresses it up.

¾ cup all-purpose flour

¼ teaspoon baking powder

¼ teaspoon baking soda

¼ teaspoon ground cinnamon

　 Dash salt

　 Dash ground allspice

¼ cup shortening

2 tablespoons brown sugar

1 egg

3 tablespoons molasses

¼ cup boiling water

2 tablespoons snipped dried cherries or mixed dried fruit bits

2 teaspoons finely chopped crystallized ginger

¾ cup whipped cream (optional)

1 teaspoon finely shredded lemon peel (optional)

Generously grease the bottom and halfway up the sides of a 1-pint straight-sided, wide-mouth canning jar. Flour the jar; set aside. In a bowl stir together flour, baking powder, baking soda, cinnamon, salt, and allspice. In a mixing bowl beat shortening and brown sugar with an electric mixer on medium speed until combined. Add egg and molasses. Beat 1 minute more. Alternately add flour mixture and boiling water, beating on low speed after each addition. Stir in cherries or fruit bits and ginger. Pour into prepared canning jar. Cover jar tightly with greased foil, greased side down. Place in a 3½- or 4-quart crockery cooker. Pour 1 cup water around the jar.

Cover; cook on high-heat setting 1¾ hours or until a toothpick inserted near the center comes out clean. Remove jar from cooker; cool 10 minutes. Using a small spatula, loosen bread from sides of jar; remove from jar. Cool 20 minutes on a wire rack. Cut bread into 12 slices; place 2 slices on a dessert plate. If desired, combine the whipped cream and lemon peel; top each serving with whipped cream mixture.

Makes 6 servings • Prep time: 20 minutes

Nutrition facts per serving: 189 calories, 10 g total fat (2 g saturated fat), 36 mg cholesterol, 104 mg sodium, 24 g carbohydrate, 1 g fiber, 3 g protein. Daily Values: 3% vitamin A, 3% calcium, 9% iron.

Gingered Fruit Sauce

This ginger-spiked fruit sauce can be as versatile as you like. Choose several types of fruit—or just one. Serve over ice cream or angel food or pound cake.

In a 3½- or 4-quart crockery cooker combine desired fruit, apricot nectar or orange juice, brown sugar, tapioca, orange peel, and gingerroot.

Cover; cook on low-heat setting for 4 to 5 hours or on high-heat setting for 2 to 3 hours. Add cherries; let stand, covered, for 10 minutes. If desired, serve over ice cream and sprinkle with slivered almonds.

Makes 8 servings • Prep time: 25 minutes

Nutrition facts per ½-cup serving: 134 calories, 0 g total fat (0 g saturated fat), 0 mg cholesterol, 4 mg sodium, 34 g carbohydrate, 3 g fiber, 1 g protein. Daily Values: 33% vitamin A, 45% vitamin C, 1% calcium, 3% iron.

6 cups assorted thinly sliced fruit, such as peeled mangoes, apricots, peaches, pears, apples, and/or unpeeled nectarines

¾ cup apricot nectar or orange juice

¼ cup packed brown sugar

1 tablespoon quick-cooking tapioca

1 teaspoon finely shredded orange peel

1 teaspoon grated gingerroot

½ cup dried cherries

Vanilla ice cream (optional)

Toasted slivered almonds (optional)

The Multi-use Cooker

During the holidays, oven and rangetop space fills up pretty quickly. Pull out your crockery cooker to make festive desserts like those found in this book. Your cooker also is handy for "baking" breads and cooking vegetable side dishes. Also you can use your cooker for potlucks. Carry side dishes and desserts in your cooker to the party; then plug it in to keep food warm.

Your finicky family will love this spin on one of their favorite foods. Serve this pizza-flavored fondue for a graduation party or a birthday party.

Supreme Pizza Fondue

4 ounces bulk Italian sausage

1 small onion, finely chopped

1 clove garlic, minced

1 30-ounce jar meatless spaghetti sauce

1 cup sliced fresh mushrooms

⅔ cup chopped pepperoni or Canadian-style bacon

1 teaspoon dried basil or oregano, crushed

½ cup sliced pitted ripe olives (optional)

¼ cup chopped green sweet pepper (optional)

Dippers such as focaccia bread or Italian bread cubes, mozzarella or provolone cheese cubes, or cooked tortellini or ravioli

In a large skillet cook the sausage, onion, and garlic until meat is brown. Drain off fat.

In a 3½- or 4-quart crockery cooker combine spaghetti sauce, mushrooms, pepperoni or Canadian-style bacon, and basil or oregano. Stir in the meat mixture.

Cover; cook on low-heat setting for 3 hours. If desired, stir in ripe olives and sweet pepper. Cover; cook on low-heat setting for 15 minutes more. To serve, spear the dippers with fondue forks and dip into the fondue.

Makes 10 servings (about 5½ cups) • Prep time: 20 minutes

Nutrition facts per serving (with cheese and tortellini dippers): 254 calories, 12 g total fat (4 g saturated fat), 39 mg cholesterol, 738 mg sodium, 24 g carbohydrate, 0 g fiber, 13 g protein. Daily Values: 18% vitamin A, 31% vitamin C, 15% calcium, 11% iron.

Putting Cooking on Hold

Have there ever been times when you were concerned about not returning home until well after your crockery cooker dinner was finished? There's an easy remedy: Use an automatic timer, purchased at a hardware store, to start the cooker. When using a timer, be sure all ingredients are well-chilled when you place them in the cooker. Never use this method with frozen fish or poultry. Also, the food should not stand for longer than 2 hours before cooking begins.

For a fall open house, serve this meat-filled chili. Offer several toppers—so guests can personalize their chili—such as olives, tortilla chips, or sour cream.

Hearty Beef Chili

In a 6-quart crockery cooker combine both cans of undrained tomatoes, vegetable or tomato juice, chili powder, cumin, oregano, and garlic. Stir in the meat, onion, celery, and sweet pepper.

Cover; cook on low-heat setting for 8 to 10 hours or on high-heat setting for 4 to 5 hours. If using low-heat setting, turn to high-heat setting. Stir in the beans; cook 15 minutes more. Spoon into bowls. If desired, serve with toppers.

Makes 10 servings • Prep time: 20 minutes

Nutrition facts per serving: 224 calories, 6 g total fat (2 g saturated fat), 49 mg cholesterol, 807 mg sodium, 24 g carbohydrate, 6 g fiber, 24 g protein. Daily Values: 16% vitamin A, 66% vitamin C, 7% calcium, 28% iron.

1 29-ounce can tomatoes, cut up

1 10-ounce can chopped tomatoes and green chili peppers

2 cups vegetable juice or tomato juice

1 to 2 tablespoons chili powder

1 teaspoon ground cumin

1 teaspoon dried oregano, crushed

3 cloves garlic, minced

1½ pounds beef or pork stew meat, cut into 1-inch cubes

2 cups chopped onion

1½ cups chopped celery

1 cup chopped green pepper

2 15-ounce cans black, kidney, and/or garbanzo beans, drained and rinsed

Toppers such as shredded Mexican cheese or cheddar cheese, dairy sour cream, thinly sliced green onion, snipped cilantro, thinly sliced jalapeño peppers, and/or sliced pitted ripe olives (optional)

Plan Ahead

To save time in the kitchen before a party, prepare the ingredients the night before. Cut up or chop all of the vegetables and the meat. Combine the seasonings and liquids. Place the vegetables, meat, and seasoinings in separate containers; cover and refrigerate. The next day, place ingredients in the order specified in the recipe in the cooker. Cover, set it, and forget it until the party.

Chorizo Sausage Sandwiches

These spicy sandwiches are good for a home-from-college party or a block party. Tortilla chips, guacamole, and a pasta salad are simple accompaniments.

1 pound chorizo sausage or bulk Italian sausage

2 pounds ground raw turkey or lean ground beef

2 cups chopped onion

1 15-ounce can tomato sauce

1 14½-ounce can diced tomatoes

2 tablespoons quick-cooking tapioca

2 tablespoons finely chopped, seeded jalapeño peppers

2 teaspoons sugar

2 teaspoons dried oregano, crushed

16 French-style rolls, split lengthwise

Sliced pitted ripe olives, shredded Monterey Jack cheese, and/or mild sliced cherry peppers (optional)

Remove casing from chorizo (if using). In a large skillet cook sausage and ground turkey or beef, half at a time, until meat is no longer pink. Drain off fat. In a 5- or 6-quart crockery cooker combine onion, tomato sauce, undrained tomatoes, tapioca, jalapeño peppers, sugar, and oregano. Stir in the meat.

Cover; cook on low-heat setting for 8 to 10 hours or on high-heat setting for 4 to 5 hours. Using a fork, hollow out bottom halves of rolls, leaving a ¼-inch-thick shell. Spoon meat mixture into roll bottoms. Add roll tops. If desired, serve with sliced olives, shredded cheese, and/or cherry peppers.

Makes 16 servings • Prep time: 35 minutes

Nutrition facts per serving: 253 calories, 8 g total fat (2 g saturated fat), 21 mg cholesterol, 593 mg sodium, 35 g carbohydrate, 1 g fiber, 14 g protein. Daily Values: 4% vitamin A, 15% vitamin C, 6% calcium, 17% iron.

Index

Metric

METRIC COOKING HINTS

By making a few conversions, cooks in Australia, Canada, and the United Kingdom can use the recipes in Better Homes and Gardens® *New Flavors From Your Crockery Cooker* with confidence. The charts on this page provide a guide for converting measurements from the U.S. customary system, which is used throughout this book, to the imperial and metric systems. There also is a conversion table for oven temperatures to accommodate the differences in oven calibrations.

Product Differences:

Most of the ingredients called for in the recipes in this book are available in English-speaking countries. However, some are known by different names. Here are some common American ingredients and their possible counterparts:
• Sugar is granulated or castor sugar.
• Powdered sugar is icing sugar.
• All-purpose flour is plain household flour or white flour. When self-rising flour is used in place of all-purpose flour in a recipe that calls for leavening, omit the leavening agent (baking soda or baking powder) and salt.
• Light corn syrup is golden syrup.
• Cornstarch is cornflour.
• Baking soda is bicarbonate of soda.
• Vanilla is vanilla essence.
• Green, red, or yellow sweet peppers are capsicums.
• Golden raisins are sultanas.

Volume and Weight:

Americans traditionally use cup measures for liquid and solid ingredients. The chart, below, shows the approximate imperial and metric equivalents. If you are accustomed to weighing solid ingredients, the following approximate equivalents will be helpful.
• 1 cup butter, castor sugar, or rice = 8 ounces = about 250 grams
• 1 cup flour = 4 ounces = about 125 grams
• 1 cup icing sugar = 5 ounces = about 150 grams
Spoon measures are used for smaller amounts of ingredients. Although the size of the tablespoon varies slightly in different countries, for practical purposes and for recipes in this book, a straight substitution is all that's necessary.
Measurements made using cups or spoons always should be level unless stated otherwise.

EQUIVALENTS: U.S. = AUSTRALIA/U.K.

$\frac{1}{8}$ teaspoon = 0.5 ml
$\frac{1}{4}$ teaspoon = 1 ml
$\frac{1}{2}$ teaspoon = 2 ml
1 teaspoon = 5 ml
1 tablespoon = 1 tablespoon
$\frac{1}{4}$ cup = 2 tablespoons = 2 fluid ounces = 60 ml
$\frac{1}{3}$ cup = $\frac{1}{4}$ cup = 3 fluid ounces = 90 ml
$\frac{1}{2}$ cup = $\frac{1}{3}$ cup = 4 fluid ounces = 120 ml
$\frac{2}{3}$ cup = $\frac{1}{2}$ cup = 5 fluid ounces = 150 ml
$\frac{3}{4}$ cup = $\frac{2}{3}$ cup = 6 fluid ounces = 180 ml
1 cup = $\frac{3}{4}$ cup = 8 fluid ounces = 240 ml
$1\frac{1}{4}$ cups = 1 cup
2 cups = 1 pint
1 quart = 1 liter
$\frac{1}{2}$ inch =1.27 cm
1 inch = 2.54 cm

BAKING PAN SIZES

American	Metric
8×1½-inch round baking pan	20×4-cm cake tin
9×1½-inch round baking pan	23×3.5-cm cake tin
11×7×1½-inch baking pan	28×18×4-cm baking tin
13×9×2-inch baking pan	30×20×3-cm baking tin
2-quart rectangular baking dish	30×20×3-cm baking tin
15×10×1-inch baking pan	30×25×2-cm baking tin (Swiss roll tin)
9-inch pie plate	22×4- or 23×4-cm pie plate
7- or 8-inch springform pan	18- or 20-cm springform or loose-bottom cake tin
9×5×3-inch loaf pan	23×13×7-cm or 2-pound narrow loaf tin or pâté tin
1½-quart casserole	1.5-liter casserole
2-quart casserole	2-liter casserole

OVEN TEMPERATURE EQUIVALENTS

Fahrenheit Setting	Celsius Setting*	Gas Setting
300°F	150°C	Gas Mark 2 (slow)
325°F	160°C	Gas Mark 3 (moderately slow)
350°F	180°C	Gas Mark 4 (moderate)
375°F	190°C	Gas Mark 5 (moderately hot)
400°F	200°C	Gas Mark 6 (hot)
425°F	220°C	Gas Mark 7
450°F	230°C	Gas Mark 8 (very hot)
Broil		Grill

*Electric and gas ovens may be calibrated using Celsius. However, for an electric oven, increase the Celsius setting 10 to 20 degrees when cooking above 160°C. For convection or forced-air ovens (gas or electric), lower the temperature setting 10°C when cooking at all heat levels.